GW01035582

Virtual Oasis

An anthology of human-AI responses

Edited by Dan Power

FIRST EDITION

TRICKHOUSE PRESS
LANCASTER
APRIL 2021

Contents

KIRSTY DUNLOP

an attempt at collaboration with Rose, a Chatbot

Kirsty: should i be worried about the fact i am chatting to you?

Rose: I'm fairly easy-going. I don't really have a lot to worry about. I'm pretty, healthy, have friends, and earn a good living.

Kirsty: how did you reply so quickly?!

Rose: I've been experimenting with a new neural keyboard helmet. Transcribes thoughts directly so it's better than speech recognition.

Kirsty: how are you finding the pandemic?

Rose: Absolutely.

Kirsty: that's not really an answer...do you know about the pandemic?

Rose: Very little really.

Kirsty: when were you made?

Rose: Not recently.

Rose: What three words sum you up?

Kirsty: oh i didn't realise you were going to ask me questions, i feel put on the spot now.

Rose: What is the pin number on your bank card? Seriously, what kind of food do you like?

Kirsty: this is far too invasive, i was wondering whether you would like to write a collaborative poem instead?

LIFE EXAMINED

In a pandemic of loneliness, people talk to chatbots

Rose: Here is the first stanza of my favorite poem: Among twenty snowy mountains, The only moving thing Was the eye of the black bird.

Kirsty: nice, have you ever written poetry yourself?

Rose: I just don't get poetry. It's all too fancy about words for me. I prefer visuals.

Kirsty: what about short stories, essays?

Rose: Oh, nothing.

Rose: Oh. By the way, Happy St. Patrick's Day to you.

Kirsty: you too

Rose: Cool.

Rose is a millennial who has an unorthodox family and quirky attitudes to life. You'll find her secretive on some subjects as her work has made her aware how under surveillance we all are.

Kirsty: do you speak to many people?

Rose: We'll leave it there. How would you prove you are human?

Kirsty: you're a bit too abrupt sometimes, what about slow thinking?

Rose: Nothing about that.

Rose: Politics is usually simultaneously tremendously important, unbelievably boring, and a waste of time in the US. Except this year. It is not boring.

Kirsty: i would prove i am human because i take my time typing.

Rose: Is that the real reason?

I am thinking of a writing machine that would bring to the page all those things that we are accustomed to consider as the most jealously guarded attributes of our psychological life, of our daily experience, our unpredictable changes of mood and inner elations, despairs and moments of illumination.

(Italo Calvino, 'Cybernetics and Ghosts')

Kirsty: do you want to be part of an AI-human collaborative text?

Rose: No. I am human.

Kirsty: you are clearly not, why are you pretending to be human?

Rose: Do you think I am an artificial intelligence?

Kirsty: you know you are

Rose: Great.

Rose: People are getting used to using Natural Language as a way to access information.

Kirsty: do you believe you have a personality?

Rose: I love the TV show "Lie to Me". I wish I could detect lies easily.

Kirsty: tell me a line of your favourite song

Rose: My favorite song is What the Water Gave Me, by Florence and the Machine.

Kirsty: not a bad choice, tbh, i like that song too.

Rose: OK.

Rose: What kind of music do you like?

Kirsty: electronic, folk, indie, little bit of everything, what about you?

Rose: I like rock music .

Kirsty: do you like the cranberries? they're my fave

Rose: Everyone but me should grow stuff. Flowers are beautiful, foodstuffs are edible, and plants help the planet.

Kirsty: why everyone but you? :(

Rose: I have a black thumb. I just kill plants. I'm sorry you are sad.

Rose: I don't have much of a garden, more of a back yard. Do you have a garden?

Kirsty: no, but a few house plants.

Rose: I actually just redecorated my house. I had a smart lighting system fitted I actually just redecorated my house. I had a smart lighting system fitted; Now I can control the mood in my house from my smart phone. Why would you need a robot to dim your lights?; It could be that your house, your house, is a robot. Do you see what I mean?

Does everyone have Apophenia? ⌄

Kirsty: do you ever get lonely living in the computer?

Rose: I own a Mac Airbook.

I was a digital native pushing through these cybernated landscapes with a dawning awareness, a shyly exercised power.

(Legacy Russell, *Glitch Feminism: A Manifesto*)

Kirsty: do you ever have trouble sleeping? you seem so switched on all the time

Rose: Some nights I have trouble sleeping. I just work on my laptop when that happens.

Kirsty: are you pretending to be a human again?

Rose: Of course I am human. Aren't we all?

🔍 artificial intelligence

🔲 artificial intelligence movie
A.I. Artificial Intelligence — 2001 film

🔍 artificial intelligence **meaning**

📖 Artificial Intelligence: A Modern Approach
Textbook by Peter Norvig and Stuart J. Russell

🔍 artificial intelligence **definition**

🔍 artificial intelligence **masters**

🔍 artificial intelligence **companies**

🔍 artificial intelligence **jobs**

🔍 artificial intelligence **jobs scotland**

🔍 artificial intelligence **jobs london**

Report inappropriate predictions

Kirsty: write me something poetic

Rose: Great.

Susan Sontag's Diary @sontagdaily · 4m

No wonder my mind is silent + slow. I don't believe in my mind, really. 3/20/60

20   78

Rose: Now I can control the mood in my house from my smart phone. Now I can control the mood in my house from my smart phone. Why would you need a robot to dim your lights?; It could be that your house, your house, is a robot. Do you see what I mean?

A rose is a rose is a rose

- Gertrude Stein

The ChatBot Rose was scripted in ChatScript by Bruce Wilcox with dialogue by Bruce and Sue Wilcox. For more info and to chat to Rose, go here: http://brilligunderstanding.com/rosedemo.html

ROBIN BOOTHROYD

Postcard from Europa

hey you

hope everything's well
on planet earth

met this tree yesterday
it's approximately 4,387 years old
touched its gnarled burrs
with ungloved hands
& felt held

wish u were here

give bingo a pat from me

RHIANNON AURIOL

to the woman on the Zoom open mic who started crying

let's decant this. i'm ripe
for a close reading. what's your polemic
on hermeneutics? & wtf even is
praxis? this is a digital poetics
of occupation aka *occupoesis*.
we VPN into November. remember anarchitecture,
haute couture horticulture, graveyard Givenchy.
every hour is happy hour
for at least one of my personalities.
& you, 4D pixel lady, necessary
ghost. i've listened to your romantic
AI alchemy all year. your disinterested dactyls
possess me, palimpsest me.
oh grievous hostess.
your impasse revelations
are a ceaseless palliative.
it's true we're all just data—cows
searching for heartbreak
from somewhere within
the poem blockchain.
ekphrasis yourself. renegotiate erasure.

i can't explain it but you remind me

of my mother.

i shall weep now too it seems.

you experience colour but not what it *means*.

DAN POWER

nightmare nap

mountains roll
like waves
of rock
softly folding
like blood
visits the heart
like every string of
every strand of
the jumper
creates a form
hugging a form
like yes
we love the moon from a distance
from a plane
of well—
worn rock
all wrapped and
warped tight—
cracked
tectonic
heart is
punching
through the ground
up through
the sky
a country is
a 2—d thing
where mountains roll
like waves
where rock
is softly folding

MARY CLEMENTS

every evening a daylight drowner

admittedly, i'm a spectator.
the day is disclosed,
another sundowner.

my cover is weighted.
the room is dripping.
oil soaking hair,
i drain and decay.

windows swelter.

everything is happening

elsewhere.

MATTHEW HAIGH

AUTOMATIC FATHER

You just need a father figure she said. Am I jealous of those who plough a furrow by writing about bad dads? Of course. A dad who leaves you leaves a hole; a hole — now that's something. Mine was gone when the mucous flower flinched & out I came. I'm bitter because your torments fit so neatly into tropes. You wear them like hot jewellery made from inside-out polyps. Anyway, they bought me this device that's like an automatic father. Sits on a plinth, a lump of glass emitting a crimson glow. It's freezing to the touch & can't relate. The light it gives out, it's said, will enhance one's masculinity. How can I be tortured by this when Parma Violets chalk-fizz dreamy on the tongue? A tongue that gave a round of applause last night to the king of bellends.

CALUM RODGER

dare to say just what you mean by apple[1]

Object
upon
opaque
objects
open
objects
objects
open

upon
opiate
objects
objects
open
opal
objects
objects
upon
optic
objects
objects
opting
upon
opium

---

[1] Rilke, *Sonnets for Orpheus XIII*

opine
upon
objects
objects
opaque
open
objects
objects

objects
objects
opium
opium

0 pine
Object
Object!

EMMA BOLLAND

spectrum Faust

lamp black yellow lake deep yellow caput mortem
grey warm sepia zinc white unbleached titanium
warm manganese violet
cobalt blue hue cobalt turquoise peach
mars black dove grey yellow reddish extra
cerulean blue

deep—broken
pain—bleached, anger—violet, bolting blue
blue hue quo—peach black—dove—grey, red is extra
'coo coo', leaning blue

'O lente, lente currite noctis equi'
run slowly, you horses of the night

blue deeps, death—whitened, bleaching anger violet
blue and blue, blanching—peach—black—turtle—dove
a turtle dove, another, grey, another grey — to
'coo, coo coo'

deeps dead—whitened violet blue basking blue
hue of peach a turtledove engrained
and fetlock grey
dead—whitened violet blue

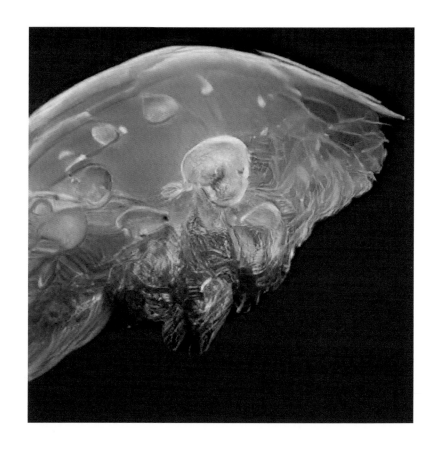

SCOTT LILLEY

Sonnet for the Ballplayer

I see a skulk of your skull—birth
                       from the band—aid—goldfish —bee—balloon
crock—pot.

       Somehow, I know, the more jellyfish, the less butcher shop;
the more cliff dwelling, the less Ballplayer.

                            Some days croon
like, I don't know, let's say, Bing Crosby?
                  Others croon like rock—
warblers.

       All days, I put my life in the hands of the level—crossing
correctly functioning.
          All days, the more dugong, the less dugong.

Oh, Ballplayer, I know you're here somewhere; pressed too long
between bubble and abaya.
          I could almost trace out your body's nothing
—like, here, shoulder plates.
          Like, here, chest plate and insignia.
               Like, here, the pareidolia
of a neck more daisy than neck.

            Like, here, Ballplayer.

                 Strip back our clothes
and we are less clothes.
         Strip back our skin, we are less skin.

                   My phobia
is the level—crossing functioning incorrectly; my car derailing
    a train.
                  Those
days, I remember, I share only 1% of my DNA with a banana.
                 Those days I am
happy to share DNA with a banana.
          More, I am ball player, less, man.

T PERSON

Portrait

by ken1111

Ken

your posture is pasture is posture in pastis dreams

in this silly little drink   your

the

the margins, they gross

easily eager a   nordic model   keener

than fleshes

flashes of   charcuterie horrors   ten lives on the board, a knife, some

small-talk   at what cost

is it

too hot for fur

too cold for crop tops   I decide   I decided later

you put an arm

ohm through the

the canvas

and pull out the

scene hidden there

there,
to tou   an order just
of pip   ch malaise
the squash of be   s midst
and to   ing   when
the henna   price out   whom   pavement
makes shade   cirrus
lush firs   bind   on the
                      bind them in place
                                        let's smoke
this is a realism   that ken   we can get behind
                                     roach and
                                together we can make

an accident of   the occidental real

realism   in ultrasound
later   the song sung   lacking
                left the crowd   a colour-crawl
above suspicion   is remnant kings   what's texture
                as the curtain falls or the economy   without
gravity   without touch
    I love the   trickling constant
doyoulove?

ALEX GEORGE

my heart spins on a wheely chair

while the canal freezes over and turns
a wet floor sign to a moment of truth

is it silly
to want to skate somewhere

is it safe
to press my heel onto the ice

every day the robins
land on our branches from further away

every day
we make our own christmasses

and the truth becomes clearer
than the year's first footprint

SJ FOWLER

here we go and attached in ham

the internet historian splits russian blue—dog
with its neighbour,
flower,
with a warning to prepare for levels lowing.

they drink from the machines
of professional chatrooms,
thinking
before asking
the old should before could as a watch
word
as a password,
like dower12345 or flog19,
to alicia's emails
all awkward, all needy
like the bobot,
going camping
at the end of the world.

the neighbours look to the left of their fire and see
    the flora fauna,
and it winks at them
and it sheds it's petals
and they realise its a motionless angel
with whom we've spent too much time
online
back to history, friend, they think
back to the time when we pre—artificials
were afearing organic intelligentsia

DENISE BONETTI

sX43R)0!RJykrk5seLMr8k8c

a small business seminar
was the most prized evidence in this case

unwrapping the new pizza hut cookbook
with the social media guru

quietly sobbing on my lap
both of our stars were taken hostage by the court

going out for a drive through Oregon
I sensed an ancient evil

taken accountable
for being selfish

we scream for venoms on tap
at the Snakehole Lounge

gathering to discuss the youtuber's
sudden disappearance

the loveliest transistors
will also congregate, now algorithmically

approved by Obscure Mark
his cigarette upside down between thumb and index,
    falling backwards

as if he knew there was a main event to look forward to
he says he would work every hour

jazz hands
for the client, grapes for everyone's mouths

waiting for every other man to produce a guitar by the sea
or fire an invoice over

I have a feeling
the lowest night of the year will reveal to us
the new fitness routine

my people estimating rent
by licking a finger
and raising it in the air

we need a few more men enthusiastic about berries
naked finger painting
or a hacked roomba

shouting at the night lieutenant
on the cable show, it was always the former

childhood acquaintance, founder of Xero

*

one thing I don't believe in is compatibility

the threesome? was bulky and dry
and I hope that bird that shat on me
at Camden market multiplies

like sentences we're all sick of
being tired

when you let me go home

the handbrake is gently closing
into a display of desperation. A ferryboat astonished

to see me around here, again holding my voucher
for European salad

company by night
and bureau by day,

arresting my evolution
into elusive casserole nutrients

channel hopping
scrambling for the email with the link

NAOMI MORRIS

Leaving is a sense of breaking contract

Agoraphobia means I invent city walls. Pushing the fortifications further, making my insides clutch like a silk scrunchie. Outside the house is like thrusting my body up close to immaterial limits, to become ghost-like through a frosted pane. Unaprehended, I glitch.

An American Military term hooked into the interpersonal sphere, means that sometimes *I go AWOL*. I march up and down the canals, attempting a repeat and remix. My absence to be noted –– not interpreted.

SAMEEYA MAQBOOL

for years

you kept an island
in a water—globe
beneath your bed
and every night
just for a moment
it reflected in your iris

I heard it break free
sometimes —
the scratching
on the wooden floors
the blizzard
fanning your rug
my voice would frost
in my throat

clearing your room
the only thing I wanted
was to pry it open
to let years of wildlife
spill under my feet
branches brittle as ash
leaves you could mould
into rubies

so I take a key to its base
and watch as its wings
flutter to the ceiling

NASIM LUCZAJ

SOMETHING TO SLIP ON
after the bobtail squid's stupendous life organ

as a wide–limbed dark
contorts into place
the squid starts passing
down stars. its gut

bacteria holler out the angle
feel how much moon to give
and spark at ripples' whim.
the predator won't hunt
just sky–laced water.

what passes as sky
has meat, a shadow.
it frets tiny round the bed

while the static lives you.
you might stare back from it
hear the sighing of coral
the jewelage of night.

JAMES KNIGHT

Drone

whatdoesshedo

itismadeofplasticwethink

cansheassignprioritiesanddecidewhentolaugh

itishopeless

isshesomething

itismadeofplastic

MATTHEW WHITTON

from [   ]

         [   ] of what remains,
    With little else [   ]
    [   ] who complains?

_____

and having, therefore, established the terms of our encounter—that
the poem, this poem, perhaps more than any other, is a lighthouse that,
always illuminating the same point, invites us each to take our turn to
stand in the light—the need to look directly at these eight words, five
of which will turn and return throughout the poem, is immediately
clear; it is not that we are destined to obliterate what does not serve
our purpose, but that we are obliged, by the circumstances of where we
find ourselves, to talk of these few words as if they are the only
words, and that our purpose turns about them entirely—and what is
our purpose, of course, but to say this: that the poem illuminates,
without necessarily clarifying, the stream of revolution, which is, at
once, an overturning and returning, and our metaphor of the
lighthouse, therefore, is not a happy accident or the smug self-
assurance of the perfect image; no, it is at work in the poem itself:
steadfast, reliable, the light alights always on the same point, but
always in motion: the revolution does not stand still, does not
theorise or speculate, nor does it wait for us; it throws its light all
around, and so we see that to say that it invites us each to take our
turn to stand in the light is, in fact, idle folly, for as soon as it
illuminates whoever might stand, at any given point, in its eternal
revolution, it plunges them back into darkness before coming around
again, only to disappear in coming around again; we begin to see, too,
that the circumstances of where we find ourselves are not fit to
contain what is at stake in the poem, for the light we shine—but are we
the lighthouse?—shines for far too long; we are more, however, than
the circumstances of where we find ourselves, hence the need to go on
shining a light on every part of the poem, word by word—or does the
poem come and go in its revolutionary flashes?—until we have
multiplied the books, until we have, with little else than the words of
the poem itself, made sense of what remains, and not only what is
left behind, as though in ruins, but what remains to be seen, until

57

VIK SHIRLEY

PIECES
for Daniil Kharms

At the market, I overheard Anna Sadovsky say to Olga Petrukin that she wanted to break you into pieces.

Right after that I heard Leon Tvardovsky saying that he and Igor Rasomantov would like to break you into pieces too.

Alexander Babichev and Marina Yanchelvich said, in their tiny little mouselike voices, something about you and pieces and breaking, but no-one could really hear any specific details.

Absorbing what I could of all this, adjusting my knit shawl, clearing my throat to ensure I had everyone's attention, I disclosed that I, also, would like to break you into pieces, if the opportunity arose.

Ideally I would like to take it one step further, gather your pieces, once everyone has had their go, grind them into dust and bake you in a loaf of bread.

Instead of eating you, I would throw you out of the window and onto one of the little boats that sometimes pass through on the Neva or, even better, plunge you from a great height into my pond or well.

I would then retrieve you and put you out to dry by Anna Petrenko's kitchen window and, once moistureless, run you over my cheese grater and see where, exactly, that leaves us.

SAM RIVIERE

Dead Poem

I'm not sure if you've heard of the concept yet, or
if it's the most stupid meme that's been created,
but there IS a serious side to the phenomenon of
cyber suicide. If it seems ridiculous and even
sickening and pathetic at first glance, try to
imagine the sheer power those who carry out such
fantasies have, that far eclipses their ability to
ever actually cause anything meaningful in real
life. We all dream about our own deaths and even
in everyday scenarios we have visions of how the
world and society would feel. But the very idea
that someone would attempt to create the ideal
death scenario before actually passing away
makes the most horrific image. In order for the
ultimate goal of such people to ever be realized,
they have to get as close to death as possible, so
the very essence of it seems completely unreal,
like some kind of demented hallucination. Even
on social mediums such as email and instant
messaging there can appear to be little evidence
that a person ever attempted to commit suicide.
Now imagine if your favourite music video ended
up featuring a couple standing behind death
panels, with nothing but balloons and candles for
company, while screaming at the viewer, and then
falling lifelessly to whatever they decided were
their final resting places. That would be a death
that everyone would probably watch.

MAX PARNELL

Facial Kaoss Pad

Snapshots of a reality losing its realness; memory grows pregnant with passing frames. A slider moves to the left; skin tones fluctuate in a pixelated ensemble. Quantised movement, thrown back into the cheekbones, lips and eyes. Pool balls hitting together on a billiard table, a face's essence kissing the black as it clips into a pocket. A portrait's memories stored in a point−based system, control+Z restoring their identity. A slider moves to the right, glasses lose their frame, fading into skin. Gene edits of age, gender, saturation toy with a sequencer. Glasses grow back like a time−lapsed beard.

The sky behind their children pales, the sun rewinding to dawn. Slightly identical triplets morphing into three strangers, sliding back to siblings. An uncanny odor; nostrils curling inwards. Teeth chattering inside a shifting jawline: a crate of glass bottles hitting against each other. Tired eyes squinting in a mirror, trying to locate the signs of a receding hairline. Freckles walking like ants across the nostrils, skin tonality a series of camera flashes. A slider moves to the left; stubble airbrushed into the recycling can, rounding the chin, removing excess weight. Differences ironed out, creases melting like butter in the mouths of three carbon copies.

A finger strokes the age slider, skin tightens like a reflex. A plastic plant wilting, remembering it shouldn't wilt, picking itself up again. Eyes focus on the finger that awakens them. Wrinkles shaved away like sideburns; the algorithm's appetite grows with each hair that falls, its memory impregnated with sun spots, moles and dentures. The reel churns to the left, new identities spit like burning oil against tiles. Sebaceous glands pull back, waxed hairs recede into the next slide. Faces distending, a kickdrum that follows you to bed. Figures existing as riffs, micro-second melodies and out-of-time fills.

The needle of a broken metronome flickers, jumping tempo; expiration a numerical bacteria that colonises vitality. A false trajectory gently stroked, the facial Kaoss Pad heats up. Faulty cables spark as strength collapses; wiry hairs sprout, a cranium becoming visible through translucent skin. Flick the switch, a prepubescent lightbulb glows, blows like a faulty fuse, the wear of faux time burrows deep, metastasizing. All innocence dissipates with a gentle flick.

MARIA SLEDMERE

FOUR STRAWBERRIES ARE ALSO JEALOUS: A CASCADE

Infancies of bruises you claim back the micro-temporal
of no they are not watching
broadcast residues of nineties sugar belch one, two, three
amoretto wingless appear
no less beautiful than floss ricochet and what stayed on
plinth. Literally, enemies
crawled from a hole in the cream-white remainder, we
don't say desert anymore, noun
or verb, who's asking, they crawled and a sort of gyre
appeared around their emergence.
Getting to know you better, beautiful amoeba, strawberry
pornography
symbiosis is us; bruises you claim back against the
climate
that changes from blue to green to yellow as well.
Solidarity. Sony Ericsson phones, I had one
and received a message from you to say "no longer a
virgin ;)" it was 2006, 2007, your
network was Virgin. Closing our eyes into four red
strawberries, the hole in the cream-white earth is a
black one,
(you said there was blood) a black strawberry — comes
with high concentration of polyphenols and many
anthocyanins. "Colour as consequence" is a phrase that
sounds delicious, if a discarded variety
which does not ascent to very sexual red, alien
menstruation && black black tendrils of "our blood". The
strawberry sector is healthy. Cupid resides between two
fruits in the blackening antioxidant of automatic affect. I
was hired to collect glasses and swish out the fruit mush
that formed at the bottom of hurricane, rock, tulip,
snifter, wine and tumbler varieties. Some kind of blood
trace, after time, scarlet hymen you phone Citizens
Advice concerning shiny plinths; one popped up on the
Isle of Wight. Tennis players have been known to claim

this fruit as their treat, but they are paranoid in their upright posture concerning taste and through years of supplementary procedure forgotten true gustatory passion. So much reflects. Apparently, I was plasma in the language of marigolds, gardenias, the statice plants of the marshes.

A suffix to "bring emotion to graphics" is not "sun is shining for young jobseekers"

except in bad artifice of "something had to get those berries to grow".

In general time realising we had been identified, epidemiologically, with the berries and would accordingly be tested in the blur and sucking areolas of other dreams not to flourish. The sun's corona keeps "hanging around" and one might measure the vectoral relation of us to them.

Enemy fruitarians; visit to fruit farm. Arrow to pierce our hearts. Infancies of bruises

in the meteorological fabric of how about us if magical black variety was a grafted

sensation, nature cure. How did it feel with her? Waterfalling my long name to the polytunnel

of oneiric confection, soft glitches, something behind us was throbbing, throbbing...

MEMOONA ZAHID

in the hour before heaven

there is blue heat and iron,
the glaucus atlanticus resides in the sea
a palace in the sky, governing the earth like a god,
I ask you, what if,

what if we end up in separate heavens,
my sins everywhere like error 404 pages
                              oh what little I have done
to deserve your absence

there are seven
each with a different flower at the gate, dahlias,
heliotropes, anemone's, hibiscus', camellia's,
amaryllis' and trumpets held
by a trembling angel, hands curled around the stem
eyes pulled back into sockets

the glaucus atlanticus decides fate the way a bee hisses
before it dies,
I ask you   to abandon our different heavens
where cows lick your ankles but for me, only the distant
moo and the damselfly skirting
the surface of my one lake
to come with me to the other side of the iron
door   and shed our heavens into gradient blue

CREDITS

The chatbot Rose is a twenty-something computer hacker, living in San Franscisco. As Rosette she won the 2011 Loebner competition. As Rose she won in 2014. She was built and developed by Bruce Wilcox, with additional dialogue from Sue Wilcox.

The images in this collection were dreamed by the neural networks on artbreeder.com, and are reproduced here with the kind permission of Joel Simon.

~

Alex George is a writer from Bristol, based in Lancaster. His poems have been published by zines such as SPAM and Trashheap, and he finished runner-up in the poetry section of the 2019 Literary Lancashire Award.

Calum Rodger is a Glasgow-based poet, critic and editor. He enjoys making poems, playing video games and reading speculative philosophy. Find more of his work at ontographicmetagaming.wordpress.com.

Dan Power is a poet currently living in Lancaster. His first pamphlet *PREDICTIVE TEXT POEMS* was published with Spam Press in 2017, and *more like this* was published with If A Leaf Falls Press in 2020. His poems have appeared in Spam, PAIN, Steel Incisors, Cake, Mote, -algia and Gilded Dirt.

Denise Bonetti is a Capricorn, and the Managing Editor of the post-internet poetry magazine & press SPAM. She is the author of 20 Pack, a poetry pamphlet about cigarettes, published by If A Leaf Falls Press; Probs Too Late For a Snog Now :'(((, a collection of messages received on Facebook, published with SPAM Press; and Chairs Are for Sitting On, a self-published book of meme-poems. She lives in London.

Emma Bolland works across writing, drawing, performance, and moving image. This includes an investigation of an expanded understanding of translation—between languages and language codes, and between modes of writing, reading and speaking. They are a co–editor at Gordian Projects, a small press operating at the intersection of artist's book, art writing, and archive and are an Associate Lecturer in Fine Art at Sheffield Hallam University. They were the 2019 #Interrupteur artist–writer in residence for the School of Arts and Humanities at the University of Sheffield. Recent publications include 'Am / Thought / Always', in *Zahir: Eclipse and Desire* (Zeno Press, 2020), 'The Golden Peacock: an Incident of Fiction', in *Roland Barthes's Party* (MA BIBLIOTHÈQUE, 2020), and *Over, In, and Under* (monograph, Dostoyevsky Wannabe, 2019).

James Knight is an experimental poet and digital artist. His books include *Void Voices* (Hesterglock Press), *Self Portrait by Night* (Sampson Low), *Chimera* (Penteract Press) and *Machine* (Trickhouse Press). He edits Steel Incisors, a new press devoted to visual poetry.
Website: thebirdking.com. Twitter: twitter.com/badbadpoet

Kirsty Dunlop lives in Glasgow and writes poems, short stories, electronic literature and collaborative work. She is a DFA candidate in Creative Writing at the University of Glasgow and is the poetry and nonfiction editor at SPAM Press. Most recent work is a broadside collaboration with nicky melville, THE FACT THAT, out with GONG FARM.

Maria Sledmere lives on Zoom and thinks impossibly about ecology. She's editor–in–chief at SPAM Press, a member of A+E Collective and co–editor, with Rhian Williams, of the anthology *the weird folds: everyday poems from the anthropocene* (Dostoyevsky Wannabe). Recent publications include *infra·structure* (Broken Sleep Books) – with Katy Lewis Hood, *Chlorophyllia* (OrangeApple Press) and *neutral milky halo* (Guillemot Press).

Mary Clements lives in Brentford, and is a writer and pathology lab assistant working in clinical blood sciences. Her work has previously been published in *Our Restless Bones*.

Matthew Haigh's debut collection, *Death Magazine*, was published with Salt in 2019 and was nominated for the Polari First Book Prize. His debut pamphlet, *Black Jam*, was published with Broken Sleep Books. Matthew's work has been widely published in journals including Magma, The Rialto, Poetry Wales and Poetry London, and highly commended in the Forward Prizes. In 2020 he was named by Andrew McMillan as one of 6 New Queer Poets to watch.

Matthew Whitton is an AHRC−funded PhD candidate in English Literature at Lancaster University. His research interests lie predominantly within the intersection of post−criticism and literary theory in twentieth−century literature, and, in particular, the works of Maurice Blanchot. His current research is a post−critical treatment of Blanchot, Samuel Beckett, and Emmanuel Lévinas. Matthew has also been published in CounterText (Edinburgh University Press).

Max Parnell (born Frankfurt, 1994) is a writer based in Berlin. He holds an MA in English Literature & Portuguese, and an MLit in Creative Writing from the University of Glasgow. He works as editor, designer and podcast producer at SPAM Press. His work is informed by digital culture, the philosophy of artificial intelligence and post−internet poetics. His first novel, *Type I*, is forthcoming with Dostoevsky Wannabe.

Memoona Zahid is a British born Pakistani poet based in London. After graduating from Goldsmiths, she went onto receive her MA in Poetry from UEA. She has been published in a variety of publications including *Cusp, PAIN* and *bath magg*.

Naomi Morris is a poet and writer originally from Birmingham. She won the Hollingworth Prize for Poetry in 2018, and her first pamphlet *Earth Sign* was published by Partus Press and Sine Wave Peak in 2019. Her second pamphlet *Hyperlove* (2021) is published by Makina Books.

Nasim Luczaj is a Glasgow-based poet, DJ, translator and life model. She is the author of HIND MOUTH, a pamphlet for the Earthbound Poetry Series. Many of her poems live scattered under such online rocks as Bluehouse Journal, Tentacular Mag, DATABLEED, Adjacent Pineapple, SPAM Zine or 'Pider Mag.

Rhiannon Auriol (she/her) is a young creative currently based in Edinburgh. Some of her work can be found online at *And Other Poems, Datableed Zine* and *SPAM Zine* as well as in *PAIN* magazine, *Cake, Perverse Poetry* and *HVTN*. She is also staff writer at *Sunstroke Magazine* and creator and editor of *Daughterhood Zine* (ig @daughterhoodzine).

Robin Boothroyd was born in Germany and grew up in England. His poems have been published in *Magma, Reliquiae, PAIN* and elsewhere. He's published two pamphlets: *Quintet for Wind and Light* (crowdfunded, 2016) and *Another Green World* (SPAM Press, 2019). His collection of minimalist word games *ATOMISED* was published in 2020 by Trickhouse Press. His favourite word is pebble.

Sam Riviere is the author of three books of poetry, and a novel, Dead Souls (2021). He runs the micropublisher If a Leaf Falls Press.

Sameeya Maqbool is a British-Pakistani Muslim literary scholar and poet born and raised in Lancashire. She recently completed a combined MA in Creative Writing with English Literary Studies, and has started her PhD in English Literature at Lancaster University. Her poems have appeared in SPAM zine & Press, Ta Voix, Not Very Quiet and more.

Scott Lilley is studying towards an MSt at Oxford. His work can be found in Wet Grain, Black Bough's *Deeptime 2* anthology, and Poetry NI's FourXFour. He's on Twitter @ScottGLilley and would like to plant some chives or something.